CONTENTS

	2
	4
TOUR OF THE HALL	
THE ENTRANCE HALL	6
THE MAIN STAIRCASE	10
THE TAPESTRY ROOM	12
THE LIBRARY	14
THE DINING ROOM	18
THE BEDROOM	20
THE NURSERY	22
THE WASH HOUSE	23
THE KITCHEN	24
THE BUTTERY, CRAFT CENTRE & GIFT SHOP	26
EDUCATION AT EYAM	28
EYAM HALL GARDENS	30
WEDDINGS AT EYAM HALL	32
EYAM AND THE PLAGUE	34
TOUR OF THE VILLAGE	
THE PARISH CHURCH OF ST. LAWRENCE	42
WAKES WEEK	46
EYAM MUSEUM	47
MAP OF EYAM	48

Robert and Nicola Wright,
owners of Eyam Hall

The Wright family tree can be seen
in the Dining Room

WELCOME TO EYAM HALL

We would like to welcome you to Eyam Hall and this beautiful village whose tragic history attracts so many visitors.

Robert and I moved to Eyam Hall in 1990 and quickly realised that we needed to make some major changes if the house was to survive into the 21st century.

Gone were the days when the Hall estate could support the house. Much of the land and the better houses had been sold during Charles's lifetime and most of the outbuildings surrounding the Hall lay derelict. Even the remaining cottages and the Hall itself needed urgent and expensive repairs and inheritance tax threatened the continued existence of the Wright family seat.

Robert and I made the inevitable decision that the house would need to open to the public and would be run as a family business with every opportunity explored to get the house back on its feet and help it stay there.

Eyam Hall is not a museum. It is not a snapshot of the past but a living and breathing family home which has evolved over the centuries. Our present family possessions sit alongside objects and furniture which have been here for over 300 years.

We are delighted that you have chosen to visit our beautiful home and very happy to share our pleasure in it with you.

Opposite: 1918 postcard of Eyam Hall

To approach Eyam Hall through the gate and cross the formal courts to the imposing facade is to step into a bygone era. The exterior of the Hall along with the walled garden to the east, with its banqueting house, has altered very little since its creation over 300 years ago. The kitchen wing to the west of the house was added in about 1700. The Stable Block to the west of the house has found a new use as a restaurant - 'The Buttery'.

Thomas Wright, second son of William Wright of Great Longstone, built the house for his son John in 1671. John was to marry a local heiress, Elizabeth Kniveton, who exercised considerable influence over the design of the house. Although she may have been headstrong she was also romantic - Elizabeth's and John's initials can be seen on the lead downspout to the right of the terrace.

THE WRIGHTS OF GREAT LONGSTONE AND EYAM

WILLIAM WRIGHT
of Gt. Longstone *(d.1641)*
From whom are descended the Wrights of Gt. Longstone until the line dies out in 1771 and John wright of Eyam inherits both estates

ROBERT LE WRIGHT
of Gt. Longstone
(alive 1330)

MANY GENERATIONS

WILLIAM WRIGHT
of Gt. Longstone, Gent.

THOMAS WRIGHT
of Unthank, Gent.
(d.1673)

JOHN WRIGHT — **ELIZABETH KNIVETON**
of Eyam, Gent.
(1648-1693)

THOMAS WRIGHT — **SUSANNA WILKINSON**
of Eyam, Gent.
(1674-1704)

JOHN WRIGHT Esq. — **JANE FAREWELL**
of Eyam & later Gt. Longstone
(1700-1780)

Major **JOHN WRIGHT**
(1724-1779)

ROBERT WRIGHT Esq. — **ELIZABETH GROSSETT**
of Gt. Longstone
(1731-1803)

JAMES FAREWELL WRIGHT Esq. — **JANE SISUM**
of Eyam
(1738-1805)

JOHN THOMAS WRIGHT Esq.
of Lympstone, Devon
(1762-1838)

JOHN WILLIAM WRIGHT Esq. — **ALETHEA YOUNGE**
(1771-1853)

DOROTHY
(1772-1858)

MARY
(1774-1860)

PETER WRIGHT Esq.
(1781-1862)

GEORGE WRIGHT
(1799-1868)

JAMES FAREWELL WRIGHT — **GEORGINA WHITTENBURY**
of Sheffield, Surgeon
(1800-1879)

JOHN WRIGHT — **MARY ANN RATCLIFF**
Solicitor
(1805-1881)

GEORGE THOMAS WRIGHT
(1827-1922)

The Revd. **CHARLES SISUM WRIGHT** — **CHARLOTTE ELIZABETH JARVIS**
(1840-1903)
(1841-1919)

HARRIET ELIZABETH
(1845-1915)

MARGARET JANE
(1843-1906)

WALTER HERBERT WRIGHT
(1869-1926)

The Revd. **WILLIAM PETER WRIGHT** — **CHARLOTTE WINIFRED EARDLEY**
(1864-1944)
(1869-1937)

EMILY GEORGINA
(1868-1925)

WALTER VERNON WRIGHT — **VANDA MARY JACKSON**
(1913-1986)
(1916-2001)

CHARLES SISUM WRIGHT — **IRENE YEOMAN**
Teacher
(1894-1985)
(1897-1990)

DOROTHY
(1895-1993)

ROBERT HAROLD VERNON WRIGHT — **NICOLA MARY VILLIERS-SMITH**
(b.1948)
(b.1950)

CHARLES MARK VERNON WRIGHT
(b.1950)

DAVID PIERS VERNON WRIGHT
(b.1952)

WALTER HUGH VERNON WRIGHT
(b.1956)

JEREMY JAMES WRIGHT
(b.1979)

FELICITY JANE WRIGHT
(b.1982)

TIMOTHY MARK WRIGHT
(b.1985)

4

(**BLACK TYPE** denotes inhabitants of Eyam Hall)

YOUR TOUR OF EYAM HALL

THE ENTRANCE HALL

O n entering the Hall, notice the flagstones of local gritstone, which have been lent an elegance here by their diamond layout. Above, the natural ceiling beams would originally have been plastered, hence the notching. In the centre of the room is the fireplace with its 18th century surround and mantel. In 1991 we discovered underneath it an earlier 17th century fireplace which, sadly, was too damaged to reclaim.

Either side of the fireplace is a matching pair of rare bacon settles, so-called because of their original and novel function; flitches of bacon were hung to cure in the tall cupboard section, no doubt imparting a certain 'ambience' to the area! These two unusual pieces are contemporary with the original house, being mentioned in its first inventory of 1694.

The 18th century longcase clock below has an eight day striking movement and was made by Asselin, a Huguenot clockmaker, in London. To the left is a 17th century six plank coffer of cedar wood. Inside it we discovered 17th and 18th century bedhangings. The earlier ones, thought to have been part of Elizabeth Kniveton's trousseau, can be seen in the bedroom.

Asselin Longcase Clock

Elizabeth Wright

*Either side of the settles are portraits of
Elizabeth and John,
for whom Eyam Hall was built.*

John Wright

The Kniveton family

The large portrait shows Elizabeth's family, the Knivetons, with a young Elizabeth on the right. Opposite is the portrait of Major John Wright (1724-1779), John's great grandson, resplendent in his red uniform. Major John was a military man of some repute and was Aide de Camp to General Burgoyne in 1777, during the American War of Independence. He also served in Germany for a period. His sword is to be found hanging amongst other family swords above the fireplace.

Major John Wright was a professional soldier, as illustrated by the detail, shown here.

Major John Wright

THE MAIN STAIRCASE

The origins of the staircase have been the subject of some speculation, as it appears to be of an earlier style than the main body of the 1671 house. The popular story suggests that when Thomas Wright built the house he helped himself to the staircase (along with the tapestries) from the semi-derelict Bradshaw Hall. The more romantic theory is that it was built for John and Elizabeth and the the heart pendants were designed to celebrate their newly-wed status. (A portrait of Thomas Wright hangs on the staircase, with portraits of two of his daughters.)

The cupboard on the stairs contains a display of blue and white china, including 18th century Chinese export and Worcester china and 19th century locally made Rockingham.

Thomas Wright,
the builder of Eyam Hall

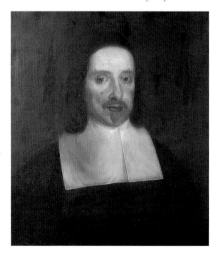

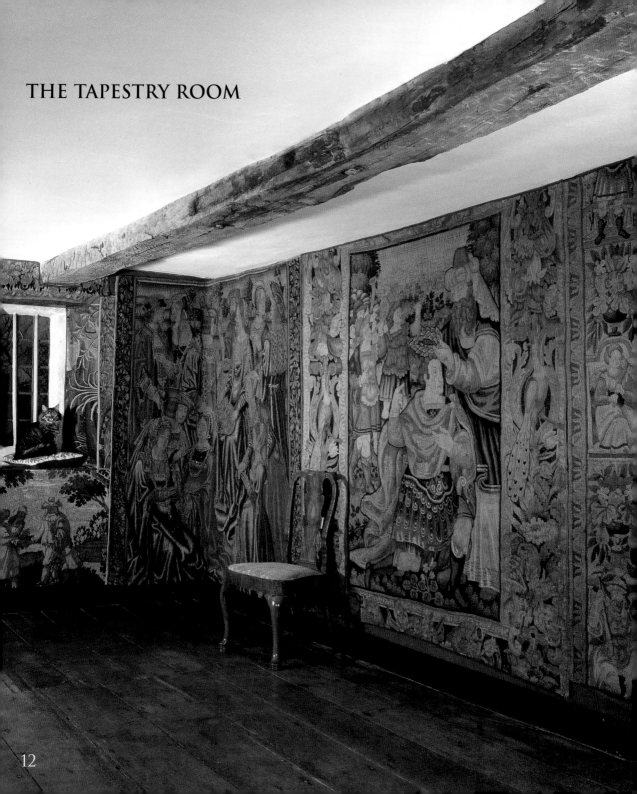

THE TAPESTRY ROOM

Whether or not this room was originally hung with tapestries is not certain, but the floor to ceiling covering you see today creates a most striking and unusual room. Rumour has it that the tapestries - in a combination of periods and styles - came from Bradshaw Hall and were hung here to keep out draughts, as well as for decoration.

The finest piece is the 15th century Flemish tapestry, worked in silk and wool, in the corner to the right of the window. It depicts a group of figures eating strawberries and other fruits from a platter. To the right are two 16th century Brussels tapestries, illustrating bible scenes of antiquity: A victorious Judith holding up the severed head of Holofernes and Jehu surrounded by his army being presented with a laurel wreath. On the wall opposite the window there is a patchwork of pastoral scenes made up of eleven pieces probably cut from the Flemish tapestry.

The early Victorian amboyna wood sewing table.

When we inherited the house the tapestries were in a sorry state. Crudely nailed to battens on the wall, damaged by sunlight and by soot and smoke from the fire, they were in urgent need of careful restoration. Whilst they underwent professional cleaning and mending, the old battens were replaced with treated timber, the walls were cleaned and the room's lighting was arranged to minimise further damage, including the fitting of ultra-violet filters over the windows. The tapestries now hang on velcro which gives them the correct support and enables them to be removed easily for cleaning.

The painting 'A Concert of Birds' above the fireplace (below), is after the style of Pieter Casteels. It, too, has been cleaned and restored, as the birds were scarcely distinguishable.

Anatomy book written by Michael Spaher, and published in 1675. The book contains many remarkable illustrations with 'fold-out' sections, similar to today's pop-up books for children.

The poem engraved on the library window is dedicated to Miss Fanny Holme of Stockport and signed R.W., presumably Robert Wright (1731-1803). He married twice, but neither time to a Fanny Holme. Whatever the true story, he certainly chose a rather public way of declaring his feelings!

THE LIBRARY

The library contains books described as a 'typical collection of a country gentleman'. Our oldest book, The Boke named The Governour, is by Sir Thomas Elyot and dates from 1546.

This room has changed both in shape and use since it was first built in 1671. Originally a great chamber, it would have led directly into the other bedrooms without corridors, thus eliminating the peculiar division of the easternmost window.

Between the windows there is one of my favourite pieces, a George II pollard oak bureau bookcase, with a fine carved and moulded swan neck pediment above a moulded dentil cornice.

The mahogany display cabinet, the elbow parlour chair, the two side chairs and the rosewood music cabinet are all inlaid with boxwood and bone and are Edwardian.The display cabinet contains a delightful Spode china tea and coffee service, c.1810.

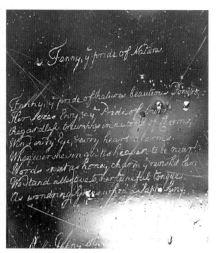

'Fanny, ye pride of natures beauteous Powers,
Her sexes Envy, and ye Pride of Ours,
Regardless triumphs in a world of Charms,
Wins ev'ry Eye and ev'ry heart alarms.
Whenever she sings 'tis heaven to be near.
Words sweet as honey charm ye ravish'd Ear.
We stand attentive to her tuneful tongue,
As wondring Syrens when a Sapho Sung.'
R.W.

THE EYAM BOOK

We acquired the 1972 Ferguson Hoey harpsichord after our arrival at Eyam Hall and, although it requires tuning virtually each time it is played, both Robert and Felicity enjoy playing music contemporary with the house.

15

John William Wright was James's and Jane's eldest surviving son and inherited Eyam Hall on his father's death. John had a mercers business in Sheffield and must have had a very kindly nature. On retirement, he bought the Brick House opposite Eyam Hall to live in rather than disrupt the comfortable lives led by his brother and sisters at the Hall.

Peter Wright was the youngest of the eleven children. Peter became a gentleman farmer and lived at Eyam Hall with his sisters, Dorothy and Mary. He was deeply involved in the affairs of both house and village, helping to set up Eyam and Stoney Middleton Association for the Prosecution of Felons and supporting the village school.

John William Wright (1771-1853)

Peter Wright (1781-1862)

Dorothy and and her sister Mary never married and devoted themselves to running the domestic arrangements at Eyam Hall for their brother Peter.

Dorothy Wright (1772-1858)

Mary Wright (1774-1860)

James Farewell Wright, one of John and Jane Wright's sons, was an equerry to George III. He married Jane Sisum in London and they went on to have eleven children, only five of whom survived infancy. Eyam Hall was left to Robert Wright's son John Thomas, who, having married well to a Devonshire heiress, had no interest in his Derbyshire inheritance. James bought Eyam Hall from his nephew to prevent it going out of the family.

James Farewell Wright (1738-1805)

THE DINING ROOM

The dining room is my favourite room and we enjoy many happy family meals in here. It was originally built as a kitchen and would have led from the hall and the back stairs via the archways. One can imagine the huge open fire – hung about with pots and pans and the general bustle of a household preparing food. When more private dining became fashionable, a new kitchen was built on the west side of the house and doors installed to create a dining room out of the old kitchen.

The dining table is laid with Victorian Staffordshire earthenware and 19th and early 20th century glass.

A Coalport porcelain dessert service can be seen on the sideboard. A collection of family silver, including some unusual engraved fishspoons, is on display.

The childrens' portraits above the mantlepiece are of William Peter Wright (1864-1944) and his sister Emily. William Peter, a retired clergyman, lived at Eyam Hall from 1923 to 1944 and enjoyed the lifestyle that would depart for ever after the 2nd World War. The house still employed a cook, housekeeper and several maids as well as gardeners and weekend house parties were a frequent occurrence.

By the time William Peter's son, Charles, moved to the Hall with his wife Irene in 1946, that golden age had departed and for the next 45 years the house had a quiet and private existence.

A meat cover

The death of Irene in 1990 precipitated the most fundamental change yet in the life of Eyam Hall. Charles's cousin, Robert inherited the house and we moved in with our young family. Once more the walls and stairs resounded with the sound of young voices and thumping feet.

Ornate wood carving on the tester bedhead

THE BEDROOM

Originally opening directly off the library, this room and the entrance lobby have been extensively remodelled.

The bedroom contains several items of furniture contemporary with the house including the magnificent 17th century tester bed. The solid roof (the tester) and bed hangings kept the occupant warm in an otherwise extremely draughty house. They also offered a measure of privacy in the days when the bedrooms were public areas.

The beautiful crewel work 17th century counterpane and curtains are thought to have been worked by Elizabeth, the first mistress of Eyam Hall, as part of her dowry. Her initials EW were discovered worked into the piece when the counterpane was conserved.

The bell pull, beside the the bed, rings a bell by the maids' room to enable the lady of the house to summon her maid during the night.

Miniature of Jane Farewell

The portraits in this room date back to the early 17th century and show various members of the Farewell family. Jane Farewell married John Wright (1700-1780) in 1721 and brought her family portraits with her. Miniatures of Jane and John can be seen to the right of the fireplace.

The Train Room
Tim Wright's impressive train layout
is on show at Nursery Halt

THE NURSERY

A fine display of Victorian and Edwardian toys and games belonging to previous Wright children leads the eye to the toys of the most recent incumbent child, Tim Wright, whose impressive train layout can be seen today.

THE WASH HOUSE

Before water was piped to the house, all the water used would have to be drawn from the well in the wash house. Our well has the dubious renown of being the final resting place of one Sarah Mills who in 1775 *'drowned herself in Wright's well house'*. All the washing for the house was done here in the original copper which can still be seen, as can the house cheese press.

The Kitchen before restoration

THE KITCHEN

The kitchen was added to the 1671 house in around 1700. It was our most exciting room in terms of restoration as we had no idea of the existence of stone arches, flagstones and a 17th century table when we first used it as our kitchen. The wonderful central stone arch was revealed when the Aga was moved to our existing kitchen. The side arches had been hidden by cupboards and plastered over. The flagstones had been covered with layers of lino and quarry tiles. The table had had drawers installed beneath it, completely disguising its shape. The stone sink was found, full of plants, in the garden. The bread oven which led into the back of the fireplace in the original kitchen can still be seen.

The gardener's family is seen sitting outside the garden house - a one up one down des.res. in the 19th century!

The Buttery serving a delicious array of home-made food, lunches and teas.

THE BUTTERY

Treat yourself to a delicious light lunch or a mouth-watering home baked cake at the Buttery. Open every day except Monday, the Buttery offers a welcome to all who appreciate home cooked food at its best. The Buttery can also be booked for private functions, buffet meals and wedding receptions.

THE VILLAGE TAVERNA

A little piece of Greece in the heart of the Peak District, Theo's Taverna conjures up all the ambience of mediterranean dining. Tel: 01433 630505

SADDLEBACK'S GIFT SHOP

Visit Saddlebacks for a range of interesting and unusual crafts and a wide choice of carefully chosen gifts. Just the place to find a present for someone special.

THE CRAFT CENTRE

Created from the historic farm buildings, the working craft centre is open all year.

THE BUTTERY, CRAFT CENTRE & GIFT SHOP

The old farm buildings have been restored and given over to modern use as a working craft centre, a restaurant and a gift shop. The craft units offer a diversity of unusual activities, many fascinating to watch. Eyam Hall licensed Buttery specialises in delicious home made cakes and light lunches. A wide variety of interesting gifts can be purchased at Saddlebacks Gift Shop.

EDUCATION AT EYAM
YESTERDAY'S CHILD
From the plague years to the present time.

A friendly and informative guide will take your party on a tour of this fascinating family home, investigating the passage of time through the eyes of the Wright family children.

The story begins when the Hall was built in 1671 and continues through the generations to the present day. Children are encouraged to compare their lives with their predecessors through paintings, costume, artefacts and toys. There is ample opportunity to handle objects and discuss their use.

The tour ends with hands-on activities in the old kitchen.

A village tour can also be organised. This offers great possibilities, not just for historical studies of the plague, but also as a study of contrasting localities for a geography topic.

Telephone for details and a teachers' pack or visit our website.

www.eyamhall.com

School Visits

The Terrace

The Garden House

Espaliered Fruit Trees

EYAM HALL GARDENS

In July and August 2004, Eyam Hall garden was opened for the first time. This traditional English walled garden contains four distinct areas dating back to its 17th century origins, the Knot Garden, the Kitchen Garden, the Bowling Green and the Lawn. Formal gravelled paths and historic architectural features intermingle with specimen trees, mixed borders, espaliered fruit trees and a beautiful rose archway.

Research and restoration have combined to return this wonderful garden to its former horticultural glory.

Planting work continues to provide a combination of historic and contemporary species and their practical maintenance in the 21st century.

A watering can 'nestbox'

'Weddings of distinction in the heart of the Peak District'

WEDDINGS AT EYAM HALL

CIVIL CEREMONIES

Eyam Hall is an enchanting family home, full of warmth and character making it the perfect venue for an intimate civil wedding (40 guests maximum). Here couples are given the personal attention and choice to make for very individual and special memories.

The Hall, where the ceremony is held, is a charming room, bathed in sunlight during the summer and made cosy by the flickering flames of a log fire in winter. Family portraits adorn the walls and two rare 17th century bacon settles flank the fireplace. The Bechstein grand piano is available if couples would like music as part of the ceremony.

The bride can get ready at Eyam Hall and make her entrance into the room down the Jacobean oak staircase.

After the ceremony, photographs can be taken in the Tapestry Room, Hall and Dining Room as well as the 17th century walled garden.

SMALL RECEPTIONS

Small wedding receptions of up to 40 can be held in the Gallery – part of the Eyam Hall Buttery – a romantic listed building complete with beams and open fire.

The elegant dining room in the house itself can be used for intimate wedding breakfasts (maximum 14 people).

MARQUEE RECEPTIONS

The garden and croft provide a stunning backdrop for a marquee reception (50 – 150 people). We can organise the whole event for you so you can relax and enjoy your special day.

Eyam Hall is licensed for civil weddings. Please ask in the shop for our wedding brochure.

EYAM AND
THE PLAGUE

In September 1665, the village tailor received a parcel of cloth from London. As it was damp from the journey, his wife asked George Viccars, his assistant, to hang it out to dry by the cottage fire. This he did, thereby releasing plague-infested fleas. After a few days of raging fever and terrible sores, George Viccars was dead. The Bubonic Plague had arrived in Eyam. Throughout the next 14 months, this horrific disease claimed the lives of 260 of the community and gave rise to one of England's greatest stories of self-sacrifice, courage and heroism.

Although Eyam has many attractions for the visitor, it is the personalities and events of 1665-6 and the physical evidence of the plague that have made it internationally famous and lent the village such a unique and fascinating appeal.

'Ring a ring o' roses
A pocket full of posies
Atishoo, atishoo
We all fall down'

This well known nursery rhyme is thought to be a reference to the plague. The "ring o' roses" was the rosy rash which developed on the victim, the posies were nosegays of sweet smelling herbs thought to ward off germs, the sneezing another symptom at the outset of the infection and "we all fall down" – death – the almost inevitable consequence.

The Plague Cottage where George Viccars lodged on Church Street.

Since about 1347 there had been frequent outbreaks of the plague throughout England, culminating in the Great Plague of London in 1665 and the subsequent fire in the landmark year of 1666.

Although there were many instances, up and down the land, of whole communities being wiped out, it is the story of Eyam that has stood the test of time and been remembered amongst all others.

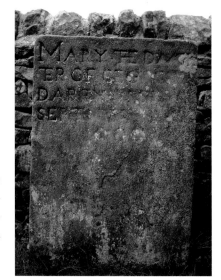

The grave of Mary Darby – one of the two lydgate graves

THE EYAM BOOK

The funeral of George Viccars took place on September 7th. His death was followed by that of Edward Cooper, the young son of his landlady. Panic took hold of the community as the death toll mounted and the pattern of disease spread out inexorably, like invisible tentacles, from the 'Plague Cottages' on Church Street. Although some of the more wealthy land–owning residents were able to flee, most of the villagers were destined to remain. By the end of October the body count was greater than the annual mortality rate over the previous decade.

'If there doe a botch appear; take a Pigeon and pluke the feathers off her tail, very bare, and set her tail to the sore, and shee will draw out the venome till shee die; then take another set too likewise, continuing so till all the venome be drawne out which you shall see by the Pigeons, for they will die with the venome as long as there is any in: also a chicken or henn is very good.. All should studiously avoid dancing, running, leaping about, lechery and bathing.'

Whole families were virtually wiped out. The Syddall family lost six out of eight members and their neighbours, the Thorpes, lost nine. By the end of April 1666 there had been 73 deaths and, aware that the plague had survived the winter, the villagers feared the worst for the summer to come. Some, such as the rector William Mompesson, 28 years old and only recently established in Eyam, sent their children to safety. Mompesson begged his wife, Catherine, to go with their children to Yorkshire but, as she felt her duty lay in the support of her husband and the community, she stayed. This decision cost Catherine her life. Mompesson decided to take positive action along with the previous dispossessed nonconformist incumbent, Thomas Stanley. In June 1666, a public meeting was held in which Mompesson and Stanley put forward three proposals:

Mompesson's Well

1. Families should bury their own dead, in gardens or adjoining fields, as the clergy were too occupied elsewhere administering to the sick and bereaved. Due to the desperate fear of infection, graves were to be dug quickly. In London, this fear gave rise to stories of bodies being interred before death and, interestingly, according to the author Daniel Defoe, brought about the practice of burying corpses six feet down.

2. As twelve feet was thought to be the minimum distance needed between individuals to prevent the disease spreading, open air church services were decided upon. An ideal spot was found in the nearby Cucklett Delf - a natural amphitheatre with a limestone outcrop pierced by weathered holes - an ideal 'pulpit'. Today, in remembrance of Mompesson and his congregation, an annual service of thanksgiving is held near this rock on the last Sunday in August.

3. To impose a quarantine upon the village, preventing the spread of the disease beyond the village boundaries to the communities outside. Aided by their deep Christian conviction, the villagers bravely adhered to this self-imposed rule. The villagers of Bubnell, near Baslow, provided their neighbours in Eyam with bread. The Earl of Devonshire, who lived at Chatsworth, became their chief benefactor, leaving food and medical supplies at his own expense at selected sites. Money was left in payment for other items and was 'purified' in two ways: in running water, as at Mompesson's Well and in vinegar–filled holes in stones, such as the Boundary Stone. Both of these can still be seen today.

Whatever the scientific legitimacy of these efforts they were indeed successful. The plague remained in Eyam, with no deaths outside the parish. With great dignity and selflessness, the residents of Eyam quietly awaited their inevitable fate.

 THE EYAM BOOK

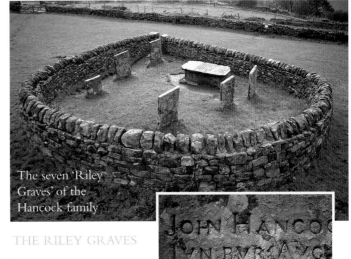

The seven 'Riley Graves' of the Hancock family

THE BOUNDARY STONE

The villagers of Eyam left coins in the holes on top of the stone which contained vinegar to disinfect them. this was in return for food which was left here by the locals of the adjoining village

THE RILEY GRAVES

By August the plague had even reached families on the outskirts of the village. One such family, the Hancocks, who lived at

The grave of John Hancock

Riley, experienced their first death on 3rd August. By 10th August Mrs Hancock had buried her husband and six children. One can only imagine the poor woman's suffering as she awaited her own demise. Three weeks later, with no symptoms apparent, she had had enough and fled to Sheffield to be with her only remaining son.

The Boundary Stone

THE PLAGUE REGISTER

After an awesome death toll of 78 in August 1666, the disease began to subside. The death of the last of the 260 victims was recorded on November 1st. Although earlier estimates suggested that there were only 83 survivors, it is now known that there were about 430. The end of the plague in Eyam was marked, as Mompesson puts it, "by a great burning" – he himself consigned to the flames everything connected with the plague, short of the clothes that he stood up in.

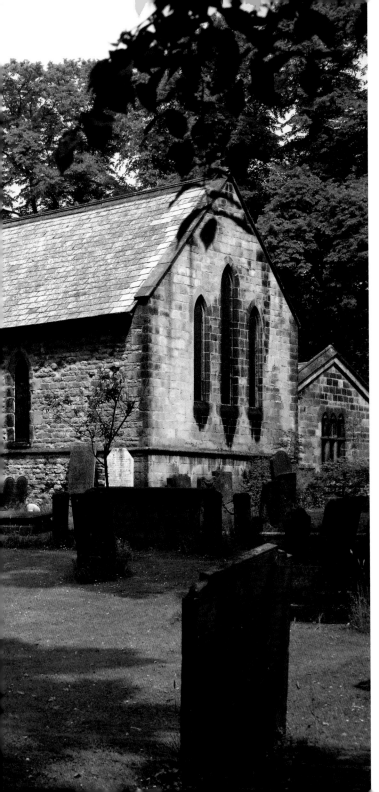

THE PARISH CHURCH OF ST. LAWRENCE

The church dates originally from the first half of the 12th century but has been much altered over the intervening years. The nave is the oldest remaining part of the church (c.1350), whilst the northern clerestory windows and the roof are sixteenth century.

By 1868, the church was in a poor state of repair and considered too small for the population of Eyam. A major restoration was undertaken which included widening the north aisle and rebuilding the chancel arch and the vestry. A further restoration in 1883 saw alterations to the south aisle including the insertion of extra windows on the south wall.

The nave paintings (c.1600), a major feature of the church, were only rediscovered in 1963, having been hidden for over 300 years. During the commonwealth period many works of art in churches were destroyed or covered up. A fund to restore these beautiful paintings was started in the village. As part of this a tea towel of the village landmarks was designed and sold, one of the main enthusiasts behind this being Irene Wright, our predecessor at Eyam Hall.

This fascinating parish church, where an excellent guidebook is on sale, is well worth a visit.

The Tomb of Catherine Mompesson

*Wife of the Rev. William Mompesson.
The top of the tomb features a curious and
corrected spelling mistake by the mason in
the carving of her name. Every year in
Eyam on 'Plague Sunday' – the nearest
date to her death and the outbreak of the
plague – a bunch of roses is placed on the
tomb by the present Rector's wife.
This commemorates Catherine's loyalty
and self–sacrifice in staying with her
husband till her death, during the
last days of the plague.*

*The mason's corrected spelling error
on Catherine's tomb.*

The Saxon cross is thought to have been a wayside preaching cross from the 8th century. Notice the carvings of angels playing musical instruments, the Virgin and Child and the rich combination of pagan and Christian symbolism.

William Mompesson's chair, located inside the church, by the altar.

The sundial was made in 1775 by local stonemason William Shore. It not only shows 'true local time' but, at noon, gives the equivalent time in places such as London, Jerusalem and Mecca. A translation of the mottoes reveals *'Take to thyself a wise mind',* on the top, and *'Like a shadow, so passes life'* on the corbels.

Eyam gravestone

INFORMATION ABOUT EYAM

A visit to Eyam's Information Centre in the historic market hall by the stocks is an invaluable source of information about the village and its history. There are information panels around the village to guide visitors and an excellent audio guide to the village which can be hired from Eyam Hall Gift Shop and Church Street Stores.

EYAM MUSEUM

E yam Museum tells the moving story of a village whose history is unique. Display areas include

The Roman origins of the settlement
The Saxon roots giving rise to the name Eyam
The nature, history and arrival of the Bubonic Plague in Eyam
Its terrible effect on the population of Eyam
The industrial heritage of the village
The geological significance of the area

The museum offers a simple, easily understood presentation of historic facts including recent research about the plague story. It is situated on Hawkhill Road opposite the public car park.

Eyam Museum

Geology display

WAKES WEEK

Held annually at the end of August, the week's events commence on Saturday with the blessing of the wells, followed by the Sunday Plague Commemoration Service held in the Cucklett Delf, to give thanks for the self–sacrifice of the villagers during the plague. Continuing a tradition initiated in 1887, the congregation and representatives of all the churches in Eyam process from the parish church to the service in the Delf. The wells at Town Head and Town End are traditionally decorated with pictures created from thousands of flower petals and other natural materials – known as well–dressings – and are blessed in colourful ceremonies. Carnival Day on Saturday at the end of Wakes Week is highlighted by the famous Sheep Roast, where a whole carcass is roasted in the open air on the old spit on Church Street. People used to make the long walk from Sheffield to sample Eyam's traditional culinary delight of oat cakes in mutton fat.

'Wakes Week'

Well Dressing

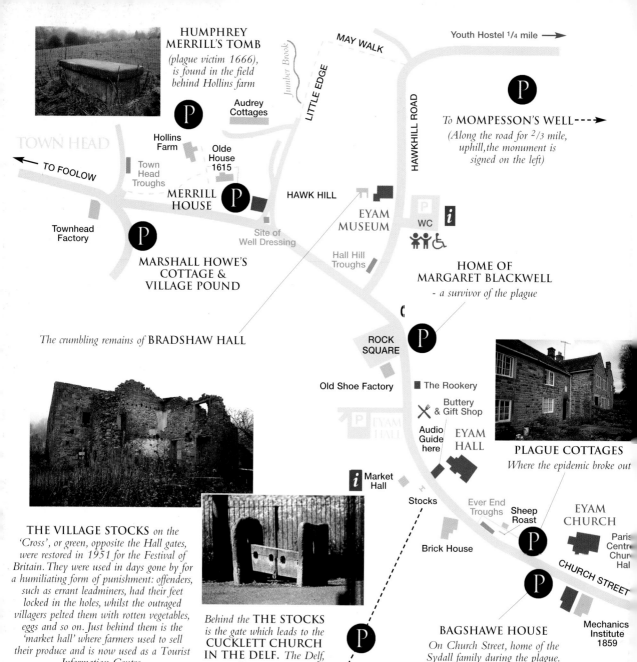

HUMPHREY MERRILL'S TOMB

*(plague victim 1666),
is found in the field
behind Hollins farm*

Audrey Cottages

Jumber Brook

LITTLE EDGE

MAY WALK

Youth Hostel 1/4 mile →

P

TOWN HEAD

Hollins Farm

Olde House 1615

Town Head Troughs

HAWKHILL ROAD

P

TO FOOLOW ←

MERRILL HOUSE

P

HAWK HILL

To MOMPESSON'S WELL - - →
*(Along the road for 2/3 mile,
uphill, the monument is
signed on the left)*

EYAM MUSEUM

P WC **i**

Townhead Factory

P

Site of Well Dressing

MARSHALL HOWE'S COTTAGE & VILLAGE POUND

Hall Hill Troughs

HOME OF MARGARET BLACKWELL
- a survivor of the plague

The crumbling remains of BRADSHAW HALL

P

ROCK SQUARE

Old Shoe Factory

■ The Rookery

✕ Buttery & Gift Shop

Audio Guide here

P EYAM HALL

EYAM HALL

PLAGUE COTTAGES
Where the epidemic broke out

i Market Hall

Stocks

Ever End Troughs

Sheep Roast

EYAM CHURCH

Brick House

P

Paris Centr Chur Hal

THE VILLAGE STOCKS *on the
'Cross', or green, opposite the Hall gates,
were restored in 1951 for the Festival of
Britain. They were used in days gone by for
a humiliating form of punishment: offenders,
such as errant leadminers, had their feet
locked in the holes, whilst the outraged
villagers pelted them with rotten vegetables,
eggs and so on. Just behind them is the
'market hall' where farmers used to sell
their produce and is now used as a Tourist
Information Centre.*

Behind the THE STOCKS
is the gate which leads to the
CUCKLETT CHURCH
IN THE DELF. *The Delf,
a steep valley, is private property
but can be visited on foot by
walking down New Close and
following the signs.*

P

P

CHURCH STREET

BAGSHAWE HOUSE
*On Church Street, home of the
Sydall family during the plague.
Emmott Sydall and her sweetheart
Rowland Torre, from nearby Stoney
Middleton, would meet in the Delf.
Once the plague was over, Rowland
sped to Eyam to meet his love
- but she was dead.*

Mechanics Institute 1859

P PLAGUE SITES OF INTEREST   **i** TOURIST IMFORMATION PANELS